FAR-OUT GUIDE TO

VENUS

Mary Kay Carson

Bailey Books
an imprint of
Enslow Publishers, Inc.
40 Industrial Road
Box 398
Berkeley Heights, NJ 07922
USA
http://www.enslow.com

For Ashley Cay Barb

Bailey Books, an imprint of Enslow Publishers, Inc.

Library of Congress Cataloging-in-Publication Data

Carson, Mary Kay.
    Far-out guide to Venus / Mary Kay Carson.
        p. cm. — (Far-out guide to the solar system)
    Includes bibliographical references and index.
    Summary: "Presents information about Venus, including fast facts, history, and technology used to study the planet"—Provided by publisher.
    ISBN 978-0-7660-3181-4 (Library Ed.)
    ISBN 978-1-59845-182-5 (Paperback Ed.)
    1. Venus (Planet)—Juvenile literature. 2. Solar system—Juvenile literature. I. Title.
    QB621.C345 2011
    523.42—dc22

                    2008050041

Printed in China

052010 Leo Paper Group, Heshan City, Guangdong, China

10 9 8 7 6 5 4 3 2 1

Image Credits: Enslow Publishers, Inc., p. 24; ESA/Cristophe Carreau, p. 16; ESA/J.Whatmore, p. 6; ESA/Medialab, p. 11; ESA/MPS/DLR-PF/IDA, pp. 1, 3, 13, 23; ESA/NASA, p. 8; ESA/VMC/MPS/IPF-DLR, p. 17 (bottom); ESA-AOESMedialab, p. 17 (top); JAXA/Akihiro Ikeshita, p. 39; Lunar and Planetary Institute, p. 7; NASA, p. 41; NASA Headquarters, p. 31; NASA/JPL, pp. 4–5, 18, 32, 35 (right), 36, 37; NASA/JPL/USGS, pp. 30, 35 (left); NASA/JPL-Caltech, p. 42; NASA/National Space Science Data Center, p. 27.

Cover Image: ESA/MPS/DLR-PF/IDA
The cover image is a map of Venus, created by the space probe **Magellan***. Reddish areas are mountains and bluish areas are valleys.*

CONTENTS

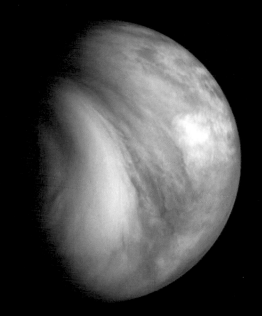

Venus

VENUS is the second planet
from the Sun. (The planets'
distances are not shown to scale.)

INTRODUCTION

Venus is often called Earth's twin. The two planets formed next to each other, and are made up of similar materials. Earth and Venus are also each other's closest neighbors, and are about the same size. If Earth were a basketball, Venus would be a slightly smaller soccer ball.

Venus and Earth are both terrestrial planets, with land and air. If you hiked around on Venus, you would see rocky mountains and valleys. (Wearing a Venus-proof space suit would be required, of course.) Gravity is not much different on Venus. You would only weigh a few pounds less there than

THIS illustration shows what you might see if you were hiking on Venus.

on Earth. But your Venus hike would *feel* very different. It would be like walking on the bottom of a deep ocean! Venus's air is so thick, it is superheavy. The heavy weight of Venus's air pushes down, creating extreme pressure. The air pressure on Venus is about 90 times that on Earth. It is equal to having nearly a kilometer (3,000 feet) of water on top of you.

INTRODUCTION
★

VENUS vs. EARTH

	VENUS	EARTH
Diameter	12,104 kilometers (7,521 miles)	12,756 kilometers (7,926 miles)
Volume	928,400,000,000 kilometers^3	1,083,200,000,000 kilometers^3
Mass	4,868,500,000,000 trillion kilograms	5,973,700,000,000 trillion kilograms
Gravity	75-pound kid would weigh 68 pounds	75-pound kid would weigh 75 pounds
Average Distance from Sun	108,208,930 kilometers (67,237,910 miles)	149,597,890 kilometers (92,955,820 miles)

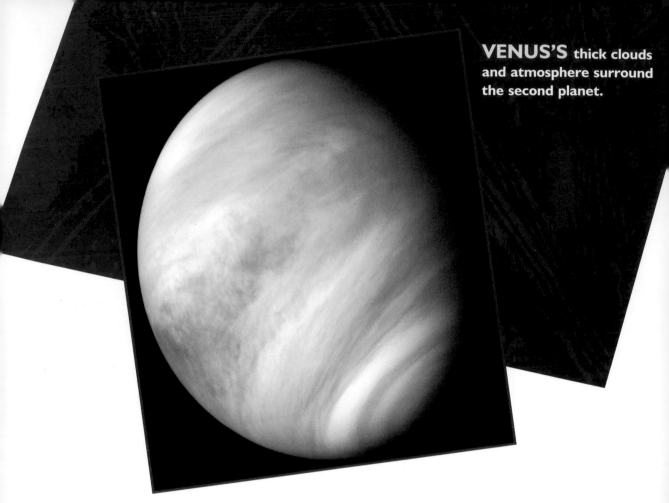

VENUS'S thick clouds and atmosphere surround the second planet.

NIGHTMARE WEATHER

Crushing air pressure is not the only un-Earthly thing about Venus. The weather on Venus is nightmarish. The always-orange sky is topped in spinning clouds that flash with lightning. Some of the clouds are yellow from sulfuric acid. This same chemical is in battery acid! The thick air under the acid clouds is not any friendlier. Carbon dioxide makes up most of Venus's air. That is the polluting gas that comes out of car tailpipes and factory smokestacks. And then there is Venus's extreme heat.

Venus is really hot. The second planet from the Sun is hot enough to melt some metals. Venus's average temperature of 462°C (864°F) turns lead, tin, and zinc into liquids. In fact, Venus is the hottest planet in our solar system. Mercury is closer to the Sun than Venus, but Venus is hotter. How did Venus get so blazing hot? It is a question scientists have worked hard to understand. The answer can give us clues about the future of Venus's twin—Earth.

FAR-OUT FACT

REALLY LONG DAYS

Imagine a world where days are longer than years. Venus is just such a place! A day is the time it takes a planet to spin around once. An Earth day lasts 24 hours. On Venus, a day lasts 5,832 hours, or 243 Earth days. One trip around the Sun, a year, takes Venus 225 Earth days to complete. And because Venus spins backwards, compared to Earth's rotation, the Sun there sets in the east and rises in the west.

CHAPTER 1

EXTREME GLOBAL WARMING

Venus's atmosphere causes its blistering temperatures. The second planet's heavy blanket of air holds in heat. Venus's atmosphere is nearly all carbon dioxide, a greenhouse gas. Greenhouse gases trap heat from the Sun, like the clear ceiling of a greenhouse. Heat trapped by greenhouse gases causes global warming on planets. Venus's carbon dioxide atmosphere is an extreme case of global warming. "That's why it's [nearly] 900 degrees [F] there," explains Venus expert David Grinspoon.

Venus was not always so sizzling hot. "We know that Venus was once more Earth-like," says Grinspoon. It was cooler and had water. Then Venus went through

ROBOTIC spacecraft
Venus Express, an orbiting
space probe, arrived at
Venus in 2006.

an extreme global warming event. "We cannot tell the full story yet," he says. "[B]ut the data we are getting shows that *Venus Express* will reveal the history of water on Venus."

EXPRESS EXPLORER

Venus Express is an orbiting space probe. It arrived at Venus in 2006. The spacecraft is giving scientists clues about Venus's cooler, wetter past—and how it compares to its twin, Earth. Venus is closer to the Sun than Earth is. This is part of the reason it is warmer. Venus gets

FAR-OUT FACT

ROBOTIC EXPLORERS

Space probes are robotic spacecraft with no astronauts onboard. Four kinds of space probes have visited Venus—landers, flybys, orbiters, and atmospheric probes (see Venus Timeline of Exploration and Discovery on page 22). Flyby probes collect information and take photographs of a planet as they fly by it. An orbiter space probe goes into orbit around a planet, circling it many times. An atmospheric probe travels through a planet's atmosphere, collecting weather information as it descends. A lander sets down on the planet.

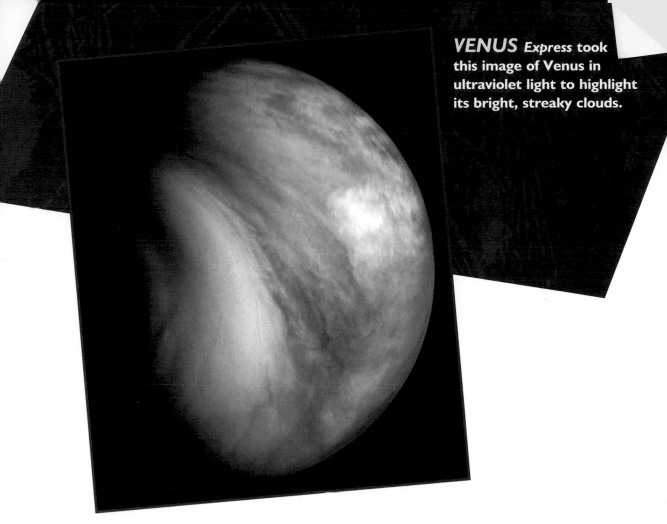

nearly twice as much sunlight as Earth. The Sun has also gotten hotter over the 4 billion years since the planets formed. *Venus Express* found evidence of ancient oceans on Venus. Scientists believe that as Venus's temperature rose, more and more water evaporated. This put a lot of water vapor in the atmosphere. "Water vapor is a powerful greenhouse gas and it caused the planet to heat up even more," says David Grinspoon.

Venus's temperature eventually got so hot that its oceans completely boiled away.

Earth is currently going through a warming period, too. Like on Venus, greenhouse gases in the atmosphere are causing temperatures to rise. But on Earth, humans are adding extra greenhouse gases through pollution. Burning fossil fuels, such as gasoline and coal, puts carbon dioxide into the air. Will Earth end up like hothouse Venus? "The global warming that humans are causing is probably not going to lead Earth to become like Venus," says Grinspoon. But studying Venus's hothouse atmosphere can help scientists understand how Earth's temperature is rising.

FAR-OUT FACT

WARMING WORLDS

Before anyone understood Earth's current global warming, scientists discovered how atmospheric gases can warm up a planet by studying Venus. Greenhouse gases explained why Venus is so hot, and got scientists wondering about our own planet. Earth has some greenhouse gases in its atmosphere naturally, including water vapor and carbon dioxide. Without them, Earth would be colder and less welcoming to life. But now extra greenhouse gases added by human pollution are overheating our planet.

VENUS EXPRESS

The European Space Agency (ESA) built *Venus Express*. Fourteen different European nations helped build the wardrobe-sized orbiter. *Venus Express* traveled to space atop a Russian rocket launched from Kazakhstan in late 2005. It arrived at Venus five months later. *Venus Express* is outfitted with seven scientific instruments and cameras. They are being used to study the planet's atmosphere, clouds, temperature, weather, and magnetic field.

FINDING LIGHTING AND LOOKING FOR VOLCANOES

Venus Express first spotted lightning on the second planet in late 2007. This makes Venus one of four planets known to have lightning. (Saturn, Jupiter, and Earth are the others.) Venus's lightning is unique in the solar system. It is the only known lightning that does not come from clouds of water vapor. Venus's lightning flashes between sulfuric acid clouds many miles above the ground. A lander on Venus's surface probably would not see any flashes. Lightning is an important discovery because it can change the chemistry of a planet's atmosphere.

AN instrument on *Venus Express* detected lightning on Venus. This illustration shows what the lightning might look like.

Volcanoes are another piece of the Venus puzzle. When they are active, volcanoes pump greenhouse gases into the atmosphere. Venus is covered in volcanoes—but are they active or long dead? *Venus Express* measured volcanic gases in Venus's atmosphere. Whether the gases came from recent eruptions or are just left over from ancient volcanoes is not yet known. Scientists want to search for hot lava or plumes of smoke near Venus's volcanoes. So far, nothing certain has been found. Venus's thick clouds still hide some secrets.

THIS illustration shows what active volcanoes might look like on Venus. Scientists are not yet sure whether any of Venus's volcanoes are still active.

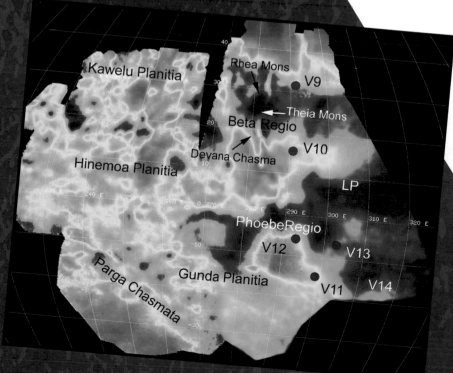

VENUS Express made this temperature map of Venus's surface. Highland blue areas are about 40°C (70°F) cooler than the lowland orange areas. Rhea Mons and Theia Mons are volcanoes. The red circles mark the landing sites of *Venera* landers (V9–V14) and the large probe (LP) from *Pioneer Venus 2*.

Kawelu Planitia

Rhea Mons

V9

Theia Mons

Beta Regio

Devana Chasma

V10

Hinemoa Planitia

LP

PhoebeRegio

V12

V13

Parga Chasmata

Gunda Planitia

V11

V14

VENUS AT A GLANCE

Diameter: 12,104 kilometers (7,521 miles)

Volume: About 88 percent of Earth's

Mass: About 82 percent of Earth's, or 4,868,500,000,000 trillion kilograms

Gravity: 75-pound kid would weigh 68 pounds

Position: Second planet from the Sun

Average Distance from Sun: 108,208,930 kilometers (67,237,910 miles)

Closest Distance to Earth: 38,200,000 kilometers (23,700,000 miles)

Day Length: 5,832 hours (243 Earth days)

Year Length: 225 Earth days

Color: Yellow

Atmosphere: 97% carbon dioxide, 3% nitrogen

Surface: Rock

Surface Temperature: 462°Celsius (864°Fahrenheit)

Moons: None

Rings: None

Namesake: Roman goddess of love and beauty

Symbol:

Planet Fast Facts

★ Venus is the hottest planet in our solar system. It is hotter than Mercury, even though it is farther from the Sun.

★ Venus's surface temperature of 462°C (864°F) is hot enough to melt lead, zinc, and other soft metals.

★ Carbon dioxide in its atmosphere causes Venus's high temperature. Carbon dioxide is a greenhouse gas that traps heats.

★ The sky on Venus is orange and has high yellow clouds made of acid droplets.

★ Venus has the heaviest atmosphere of any planet in the solar system. It is ninety times heavier than Earth's.

★ Venus is a twin planet to Earth in some ways. Venus is the nearest planet to Earth, and it is about the same size and density.

★ Venus was likely once cooler and had oceans. As Venus warmed up, all its water boiled away into the atmosphere and then was lost to space.

★ Nearly twice as much sunlight reaches Venus as Earth.

★ Venus is home to thousands of volcanoes, some possibly still active.

★ Venus's surface is mostly volcanic rock. There are steep mountains, deep channels, and some impact craters. Most of its surface was flooded with lava 500 million years ago.

★ There are two large highland areas on Venus: Ishtar Terra is in the north polar region, and Aphrodite Terra wraps around Venus's equator. If Venus had oceans, these highland areas would be continents.

★ The highest mountain on Venus is Maxwell Montes. It is taller than Mount Everest.

★ Venus has an iron core about 6,000 kilometers (3,700 miles) in diameter.

★ Venus spins, or rotates, so slowly that one day on Venus lasts longer than the planet's year.

★ Venus rotates "backwards" compared to Earth, so the Sun rises in the west and sets in the east.

★ An impact with a mini-planet-sized object could have caused Venus's slow, backward spin.

★ The thick clouds surrounding Venus reflect lots of sunlight. This is why Venus shines so brightly in the night sky. Only the Moon is brighter.

★ Venus is the only planet named after a goddess, or female god.

★ Most of Venus's features are named after goddesses or famous women. There is a crater named Sacagawea, for the American Indian guide on the Lewis and Clark expedition, and a canyon called Diana, after the Roman goddess of the hunt.

★ Venus's tallest volcano is named for the Egyptian goddess of truth and justice, Ma'at.

★ Venus is the easiest planet to see in the night sky. It is often the first point of light to appear in the evening, which is why it is sometimes called the Evening Star.

Mission Fast Facts

★ No astronauts have traveled to Venus, only robotic space probes.

★ Missions to Venus include many firsts: The first successful space probe to visit another planet (*Mariner 2*), the first planetary atmospheric probe (*Venera 4*), and the first spacecraft to send back pictures from the surface of another planet (*Venera 9*).

★ Between 1960 and 1975, at least twenty-seven Venus missions were attempted. More than half failed to launch, arrive, or remain in contact with Earth.

★ Landers on Venus have only survived a few hours before being crushed by the pressure of the atmosphere and fried by the heat.

★ Russian, American, European, and Japanese space agencies have sent missions to Venus.

★ Spacecraft sometimes visit Venus on their way elsewhere. Jupiter probe *Galileo* passed by in 1990, Saturn spacecraft *Cassini* flew by in 1998, and *Messenger* snapped photos in 2006 and 2007 on its way to Mercury.

Venus Timeline
of Exploration and Discovery

(Years given for successful spacecraft missions are when they explored Venus. This might be different from the launch year.)

PREHISTORY—Ancient peoples watch this bright shining object in the night sky.

1610—Using a telescope, Galileo Galilei studies the phases of Venus.

1927—Frank Ross takes detailed photographs of Venus's clouds using ultraviolet photographs.

1962—*Mariner 2* makes the first successful visit to Venus. The flyby probe measures Venus's temperature to be at least 427°C (800°F).

1967—*Venera 4* is the first atmospheric probe to explore another planet. It confirms a carbon dioxide atmosphere around Venus. *Mariner 5* flies by within 3,900 kilometers (2,423 miles) of Venus's surface.

1969—Atmospheric probes *Venera 5* and *Venera 6* visit Venus.

1970—Lander *Venera 7* is the first spacecraft to send back data from the surface of another planet.

1972—Lander *Venera 8* sets down on Venus.

TIMELINE

★

1975—Lander/orbiter combination probes *Venera 9* and *Venera 10* visit Venus. The *Venera 9* lander is the first spacecraft to send photos from the surface of another planet.

1978—Orbiter *Pioneer Venus 1* begins studying Venus's surface. *Pioneer Venus 2* studies clouds with atmospheric probes. Orbiter/lander pairs *Venera 11* and *Venera 12* study Venus's atmosphere and weather.

1980s—Giant radio telescopes at Arecibo Observatory map Venus's surface.

1982—Orbiter/lander pairs *Venera 13* and *Venera 14* return the first color images of Venus's surface.

1983—Orbiters *Venera 15* and *Venera 16* map Venus's surface.

1985—Lander and balloon atmospheric probes *Vega 1* and *Vega 2* study Venus's clouds, winds, and soil.

1990–1994—Orbiter *Magellan* uses radar to map 98 percent of Venus's surface.

2006—*Venus Express* orbiter begins studying Venus. It discovers lightning and active volcanoes.

2011—Orbiter *Planet-C* is scheduled to arrive at Venus after a 2010 launch and study its weather.

ace
SCIENCE
FICTION
CLASSIC
F-221
40¢

EDGAR RICE BURROUGHS

Carson Napier faces the supermen
and super-monsters of Amtor

LOST ON VENUS

LOST ON VENUS

BURROUGHS

CHAPTER 2

MAPPING VENUS

The Moon is the only object in Earth's night sky that is brighter than Venus. People have admired Venus's loveliness for thousands of years. Humans have long aimed telescopes at Venus, too (see Phases of Venus on page 26). Viewing Venus through a telescope shows a world blanketed in bright clouds. Those thick clouds smother Venus with trapped heat. Venus's clouds also make its surface tough to see. No land peeks through the swirling clouds. This veiled view of Venus long fueled Earthlings' imaginations. Up until space exploration began, many thought life thrived on Venus. There were clouds, after all, so there must be rain, many reasoned. Some people pictured Venus as a tropical rain forest world full of fantastic creatures.

THIS science fiction book, first published in 1935, describes Venus as a tropical world full of dangerous animals.

PHASES OF VENUS

Galileo Galilei (1564–1642) used early telescope views of Venus to help prove that the Sun—not the Earth, as many then believed—was the center of the solar system. The Italian scientist saw that Venus went through phases, just as the Moon does. This proved that Venus orbits the Sun, just as the Moon orbits Earth. You can track Venus's phases yourself with a strong pair of binoculars. Just watch Venus night after night to see how it changes phase. (The planet-watching Web sites on page 47 can help you find Venus.)

MELTED MESSENGERS

Space exploration ended any hope of vacationing on Venus. In 1962, a space probe called *Mariner 2* flew by Venus and became the first spacecraft to visit another planet! The historic spacecraft measured metal-melting temperatures on Venus. It scanned its thick layer of greenhouse gases, too. Venus was no tropical paradise.

The first views of what is below Venus's clouds came during the 1970s. A series of probes named *Venera*

VENERA 9 took the first photos of Venus's surface (below) on October 22, 1975. The ground near the lander was rocky and dry.

MAGELLAN

Magellan was named after Ferdinand Magellan (c1480–1521), the sixteenth-century explorer who made the first sea voyage around the world. *Magellan* was the first space probe to launch from a space shuttle. The orbiter circled Venus for four years, radar mapping 98 percent of the planet's surface. *Magellan* sent back more data than all other **NASA** space probes combined up until that time. *Magellan*'s map of Venus is more detailed than maps scientists then had of Earth's ocean floor.

traveled through Venus's acid clouds and landed on the planet. None lasted much more than an hour under the crushing pressure and high temperatures. But some of the landers sent back photographs of Venus's surface. They showed pebbled plains and volcanic rocks. Was this what all of Venus's land looked like? Scientists wanted a complete view of all of Venus. They needed a spacecraft able to map Venus through its haze. *Magellan* was the orbiter up for the job.

RADAR SPACE SCIENTIST

Magellan began orbiting Venus in 1990. Its mission was to map Venus's surface. "*Magellan* uses radar to pierce the clouds and map Venus," explained Ellen Stofan. She was a scientist on the *Magellan* team. "From about the time I was 5 or 6 years old, I knew I wanted to be a scientist," says Stofan. Fun rock-hunting field trips sparked her interest in geology. A love for space exploration convinced her to study the rocks on other planets.

Magellan's radar mapped one 25-kilometer- (16-mile-) wide strip of Venus at a time. It sent images of each of these strips back to Earth. Ellen Stofan will never forget the night *Magellan* sent back its first images. "A couple of us went in at about four in morning to look at those first strips," she remembers. As she looked at the images, Stofan saw completely unknown parts of Venus. "[T]here's a sense of awe," she says. "[Y]ou're an explorer, you're reaching into new worlds that no one's seen before."

As *Magellan* sent back more images, Stofan and other scientists got to work. They put the strips together into an amazing map of Venus's surface. "It's like trying to build a jigsaw puzzle," Stofan says. *Magellan*'s Venus map is so detailed that anything bigger than a football field shows up on it. *Magellan*'s view of Venus astonished scientists.

THIS map of Venus, which was created by *Magellan*, is color-coded to show elevation. Reddish areas are mountains, and bluish ones are valleys.

RADAR MAPPER

The kind of light we use to see, visible light, bounces off clouds. This blocks the view below them. Since photographs also depend on visible light, *Magellan* mapped Venus using radar instead. *Magellan* sent pulses of radio waves down toward Venus. These waves passed through the clouds, hit the ground, and bounced back up to *Magellan*. The time between pulses and bounces—and how the radio waves changed—measured heights of mountains and distances between volcanoes. Computers turned the measurements into a map.

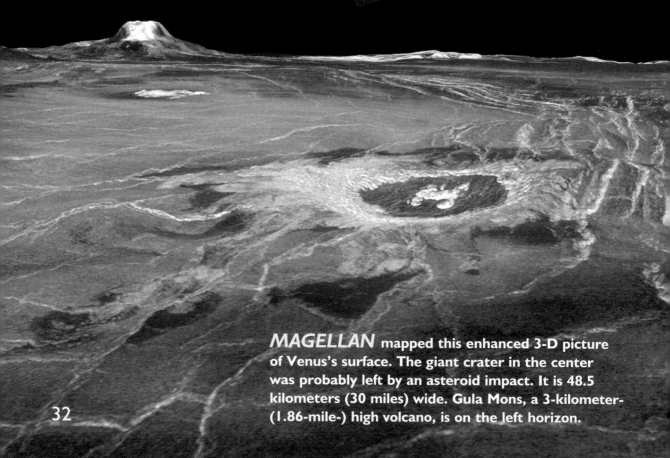

MAGELLAN mapped this enhanced 3-D picture of Venus's surface. The giant crater in the center was probably left by an asteroid impact. It is 48.5 kilometers (30 miles) wide. Gula Mons, a 3-kilometer- (1.86-mile-) high volcano, is on the left horizon.

It showed a planet with mountains, canyons, valleys, and smooth flat plains. But it is a world without oceans or water of any kind anywhere. The landscapes on our dry, hot, high-pressure neighbor were most likely created by volcanoes.

VOLCANOES RULE

Magellan revealed thousands of volcanoes on Venus. "Almost everywhere you look on Venus you see volcanic features," Stofan told reporters in 1990. Some of Venus's volcanoes and volcanic land features are similar to those on Earth. Venus has volcanoes like those that created the Hawaiian Islands. There are also giant "pancake" volcanoes, where thick lava oozed onto the surface and cooled into rock, similar to some found in California.

Other volcanic features are unique to the second planet. There is a channel of ancient lava longer than the Nile River. There are bowl-shaped places on Venus called coronae created when blobs of lava bubbled into domes and then sank. Not all of Venus's odd volcano-created structures are understood. Arachnoids are features found only on Venus. They are named after the scientific name

TICKS AND ANEMONES

Venus is full of weird volcanoes of all sorts of shapes and sizes. Some are towering mountains as high as Mount Everest. Others are flat blobs as wide as a town and surrounded by crack patterns. In fact, Venus has more kinds of volcanic features per square mile than any other place in the solar system. Scientists have made up all sorts of names for the various volcano-created landforms on Venus. Volcanoes with overlapping petal-shaped globs of lava are called anemones after the flower. Disk-shaped pancake volcanoes with leg-like ridges are called ticks.

for spiders, *arachnid*. Arachnoids look like domes with a spiderweb pattern of fractures or cracks around them. No one is sure how they formed.

REPAVED PLANET

Venus's surface also has impact craters. Asteroids that slammed into Venus probably created the craters, just like those on the Moon. The odd thing about Venus's craters is their age. None are older than a half billion

MAGELLAN mapped this 3-D picture. It is color-coded to emphasize elevations. The sunken areas are coronae, where lava domes bubbled up and then sank.

MAGELLAN mapped this enhanced 3-D picture of Venus's 8-kilometer- (5-mile-) high volcano, Maat Mons.

years or so. In fact, almost nothing on the entire surface of Venus is older than that. It seems that volcanoes completely flooded Venus with lava 500 million years ago. The lava melted and covered the old surface, leaving brand-new land. This is different from how things work on Earth. The large moving plates that make up Earth's outer covering recycle our surface. Some places are

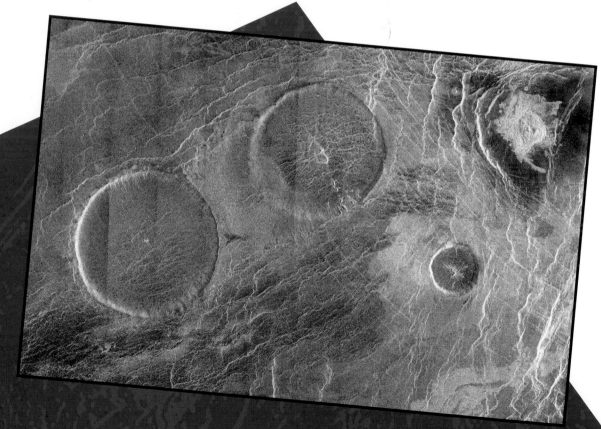

MAGELLAN took this image of "pancake" volcanoes. The two large ones are about 5 kilometers (3.1 miles) wide, with flat tops less than one kilometer (0.6 mile) high.

VOLCANOES made these "bugs" on Venus. The "tick" (left) is a 35-kilometer- (22-mile-) wide volcano. The spiderweb shaped "arachnoid" (below) is one of more than thirty identified only on Venus.

newly made, like Hawaii's newest volcanic island. Other places are ancient, like Venezuela's 2-billion-year-old mountains. Venus's volcanoes seem to remake its surface all at once. "Even though many of us believed Venus was much like the Earth," said Stofan, "Venus has turned out to be its own planet."

CHAPTER 3

WHAT'S NEXT FOR VENUS?

There is still a lot about Venus we don't know. Are Venus's volcanoes mostly dead or active? What was Venus like before extreme global warming boiled away its oceans? Upcoming missions to our twin planet hope to solve some of Venus's remaining mysteries.

Next up is *Planet-C*. It is set to launch in 2010 and arrive in 2011. The orbiter's mission is to study Venus's weather. Venus is nearly the same size, density, and mass as Earth. This means learning about Venus's weather will likely teach us about Earth's weather, too.

PLANET-C will use five different cameras to study Venus's weather. They will be able to take pictures of lightning, map cloud temperatures and chemicals, and measure surface temperatures.

PLANET-C

Planet-C, also called *Venus Climate Orbiter*, is the Japanese space agency's (JAXA's) first Venus space probe. Its five different cameras will study Venus's weather. One mystery scientists hope the orbiter will solve is why Venus's atmosphere moves so fast. Its atmosphere spins about 60 times faster than the planet itself. Winds in the atmosphere blow at up to 360 kilometers (224 miles) per hour. Scientists want to understand how—and why—Venus has such superstrong winds.

COOL LANDERS

Venus orbiters have been very successful. Lander missions have had a tougher time. The surface of Venus is just too harsh for fragile instruments to last very long. No lander has hung on for much more than an hour or two on Venus. No one has even tried sending a lander to Venus for decades. The last Venus lander was *Vega 2* in 1985.

Space scientists and engineers are now thinking about landing on Venus again. One mission being studied is called *Venus Mobile Explorer*. Its launch could come

★

sometime around 2025. The spacecraft is not designed yet. Engineers are working on creating something that can beat Venus's extreme heat.

Venus's temperatures can melt some softer metals, but engineers can build a vehicle out of materials that will not melt on Venus. The bigger problem is keeping electronics cool. High heat fries computer chips and other electronic parts. One answer could come from the kitchen. A NASA engineering team is designing a Venus

A Venus rover could study rocks and soils in different areas, not just those where it set down as unmoving landers do.

ENGINEERS work on a balloon that might someday float above Venus. Its covering reflects heat and is coated to protect it from Venus's acid clouds.

rover with electronics surrounded by a refrigerator. Cooling the rover's electronics would protect them. Another design is a balloon that floats above Venus's hot surface. It only lands long enough to scoop up some soil. Then it quickly lifts off into the cooler air again. What do you think might be a good way to keep a lander cool on Venus?

A rover would be a great way to learn more about Venus. It could help reveal the second planet's past. A Venus rover mission would help fill in the story of how Earth's twin became so different from Earth.

Words to Know

arachnoid—A volcanic surface feature on Venus that looks like a
dome surrounded by a spiderweb pattern of cracks.

atmosphere—The gases that are held by gravity around a planet,
moon, or other object in space.

atmospheric probe—A space probe that studies the atmosphere of a
planet or moon while passing though it.

carbon dioxide—A colorless gas that can be formed by the burning
and breaking down of substances containing carbon.

coronae—Bowl-shaped volcanic surface features created by sinking
lava domes.

craters—Bowl-shaped dents made by impact explosions on the
surface of a planet or moon, often from comet or asteroid crashes.

density—The amount of mass in a specific volume.

diameter—A straight line through the center of a circle or sphere.

flyby probe—A space probe that flies by a planet or moon in order to
collect data about it.

geology—The study of rocks, soils, and minerals.

global warming—The warming of a planet's atmosphere due to
greenhouse gases.

gravity—An attractive force on one object from another.

greenhouse gas—A gas that traps heat in an atmosphere, such as
carbon dioxide and water vapor.

JAXA—The Japanese space agency.

lander—A space probe that sets down on the surface of a space object.

lava—Molten rock that comes out of a volcano.

mass—The amount of matter in something.

NASA—The National Aeronautics and Space Administration, the space agency of the United States.

orbit—The path followed by a planet, moon, or other object around another object in space; to move around an object in space.

orbiter—A space probe that orbits a planet, moon, or other object in space.

planet—A large, sphere-shaped object in space that is alone (except for its moons) in its orbit around a sun.

radar—A technology or device that uses reflected radio waves to find or map distant or unseen objects.

rover—A mobile robot or vehicle that explores the surface of a planet or other object in space.

space probe—A robotic spacecraft launched into space to collect information.

terrestrial planet—A rocky solid planet with a metal core, including Mercury, Venus, Earth, and Mars.

ultraviolet light—A kind of light invisible to humans.

volcano—A break in a planet's or moon's surface where molten rock and gas can escape.

Find Out More and Get Updates

BOOKS

Bortz, Fred. *Astrobiology.* Minneapolis: Lerner Publication Co., 2008.

Elkins-Tanton, Linda T. *The Sun, Mercury, and Venus.* New York: Chelsea House, 2006.

Fraknoi, Andrew. *Disney's Wonderful World of Space.* New York: Disney Publishing, 2007.

Graham, Ian. *The Near Planets.* North Mankato, Minn.: Smart Apple Media, 2007.

Jankowski, Connie. *Astronomers: From Copernicus to Crisp.* Minneapolis: Compass Point Books, 2009.

Other books by Mary Kay Carson:

Carson, Mary Kay. *Exploring the Solar System: A History with 22 Activities.* Chicago: Chicago Review Press, 2008.

Carson, Mary Kay. *Extreme Planets! Q&A.* New York: HarperCollins, 2008.

FIND OUT MORE AND GET UPDATES
★

SOLAR SYSTEM WEB SITES

NASA. *Solar System Exploration.*
  http://solarsystem.nasa.gov/kids

The Regents of the University of Michigan. *Windows to the Universe.*
  http://www.windows.ucar.edu/

VENUS EXPLORATION WEB SITES

Jet Propulsion Laboratory. *Magellan Mission to Venus.*
  http://www2.jpl.nasa.gov/magellan

University of Wisconsin-Madison. *Venus Express.*
  http://venus.wisc.edu

PLANET-WATCHING WEB SITES

Space.com. *NightSky Sky Calendar.*
  http://www.space.com/spacewatch/sky_calendar.html

The University of Texas McDonald Observatory. *StarDate Online.*
  http://stardate.org/nightsky/planets

Index